~~100~~ MORE RULES FOR LIFE

FOR LIFE

A SPECIAL VOLUME FOR ENTHUSIASTS

REBECCA BANA

ABOUT THE AUTHOR

Kitty Flanagan is one of Australia's best-known comedians. She appears on TV occasionally but spends most of her time touring the country doing stand-up.

She has two dogs, one cat and a dishwasher that she loves more than all of her pets combined. Her favourite food is soup. *More Rules for Life* is her third book.

Also by Kitty Flanagan

Bridge Burning & other hobbies—
a collection of funny true stories

488 Rules for Life:
The thankless art of being correct

~~488~~ ~~12~~ MORE RULES FOR LIFE

A SPECIAL VOLUME FOR ENTHUSIASTS

KITTY FLANAGAN

with fellow rule-makers
Sophie Braham & Penny Flanagan

Illustrations by Tohby Riddle

ALLEN&UNWIN
SYDNEY•MELBOURNE•AUCKLAND•LONDON

First published in 2021

Copyright © Kitty Flanagan 2021

Allen & Unwin
83 Alexander Street
Crows Nest NSW 2065
Australia
Phone: (61 2) 8425 0100
Email: info@allenandunwin.com
Web: www.allenandunwin.com

 A catalogue record for this book is available from the National Library of Australia

ISBN 978 1 76106 661 0

Internal design and illustrations by Tohby Riddle
Index by Garry Cousins
Set in 10.8/18.1 pt Interstate by Bookhouse, Sydney
Printed and bound in Australia by Griffin Press, part of Ovato

10 9 8 7 6 5 4 3 2 1

The paper in this book is FSC® certified. FSC® promotes environmentally responsible, socially beneficial and economically viable management of the world's forests.

For Jazzy, my long-suffering,
rule-abiding unicorn xx

Contents

A word from the author

When *488 Rules for Life* was published, I thought I had covered everything. About a week later, new rules started popping into my head and I realised I still had so much more to give. Then Covid-19 hit and the world spiralled out of control. There were no rules for a pandemic, the government was floundering and I knew I had to step up. So that's what this book is: rules I forgot the first time, rules for the grave new world we're living in, plus some rules I considered a little too savage for the original book. *More Rules for Life* is for true aficionados, people who want and appreciate boundaries; it's not for easygoing folks with a 'whatever will be, will be' attitude. The warning is on the cover, this is a book for enthusiasts.

How to use this book

It may have been a while since you read *488 Rules for Life*—or perhaps you've never read it, in which case, interesting choice to pick up the second book first. No judgement. Either way, I thought it might be a good idea to remind everyone that these books are a joke. It seems obvious to me, but these days disclaimers are necessary as so many people have lost their sense of humour and replaced it with a sense of outrage.

So remember, I wrote the rules to entertain you, not to enrage you. If I get it wrong occasionally or if, god forbid, I offend you, there's no need to call for my head on a spike. Just turn the page. Or do what I do when I get annoyed by a book—frisbee it across the room (preferably into a wall) then stick it in one of those street libraries full of germy books no one wants. That's not only cathartic but also a truly insidious way to leave a review and make your point without shouting or raising your blood pressure.

Unlike the original book, there are no sealed sections in this volume; however, there are special 'pandemically relevant' sections peppered throughout. These are clearly marked so you can avoid them if the very mention of Covid-19 makes you want to wade into the river with rocks in your pocket, Virginia Woolf-style. Please don't do that—simply skip the grey pages instead.

And, once again, I include a tidy reminder that none of these rules should ever be shouted at anyone. If you need to inform someone of a rule breach, let them know with a wink and a smile, maybe even a friendly shoulder chuck, 'Hey, old timer, great to see you staying active but I'm going to need you to get down from there! Rule 520 says no old men on ladders. Thanks, chief!'

Always keep it courteous and lead by example. Now let's pick up where we left off at rule number 489 ...

THIS & THAT

LEISURE AND LIFESTYLE

489
Once a month, hold your yoga pants up to the light

If you can see through them, that means everyone else can too. And when I'm walking behind you and the sunlight hits your thinly veiled 'ass' at a certain angle, dear god, it's like I'm wearing X-ray specs. While the see-through look may have been charming and innocent in that first pic of Lady Diana outside the preschool, it's just plain confronting when it's out on the streets jiggling in front of my face. This is not fat-shaming, because I don't care how much junk you have in your trunk as long as it's covered by a generous thread count. Yoga pants should not provide a window to your soul.

490
Keep your mouth closed when applying mascara

Less of a rule and more of a challenge.

491
Don't go on about golf

Seriously, gents, you carry on as if this game is beyond the rest of us mere mortals. You also seem to think your clubs are delicate, sentient beings that need special knitted hats to keep their heads warm. I understand that the ball is small but it's also sitting completely still. In most other sports the ball moves all over the place, meaning you have to chase it down in order to catch it or hit it. If golf was really such a difficult sport, there wouldn't be so many old people playing it. The only hard thing about golf is finding the time and money you need to play it.

492
It's okay to say you don't like women playing football

Wait, don't jump on social media and cancel me, let me finish: it's okay to say you don't like women playing football, provided you don't like men playing football either. Otherwise, keep quiet.

493
Hunting is not a sport

Unless, of course, you're hunting a fellow hunter who also has a gun. Now you've got yourselves a contest.

HOUSE AND GARDEN

494
Match the size of your television to the size of your room

You actually do yourself a disservice by putting an oversized television in a regular-sized room. If you can't physically sit far enough away from the TV, your eyeballs won't be able to take in the whole screen. You'll find yourself constantly scanning left and right, up and down, in order to see everything that's happening. The exact reason none of us want to sit in the front row at the cinema. So unless you live in a stadium or you're planning to 'knock through' from your living room to the garage to create some distance, there's really no need for a billboard-sized telly.

495
No TVs above the fireplace

It's way too high. You'll do your neck. You want the centre of the screen to be roughly at eye level when you're seated. This means that only Shaquille O'Neal and a few other humans who are over seven foot tall should be mounting their TVs above the mantelpiece.

496
Think twice about a water feature

I'm all for an old-fashioned birdbath—it's a nice way to encourage the local birds to stop by for a sip of Adam's ale and a quick freshen-up. But once you start plumbing stuff in, adding a noisy motor and plonking a stone buddha in the middle, it starts to feel a tad over the top, and not exactly relaxing, unless you enjoy loud, electrical, humming sounds. They're also hard work. If you don't maintain your water feature properly, you'll soon end up with a stagnant, mosquito-breeding swamp in your courtyard: 'Welcome, everyone, have you seen our Zika fountain?'

497
Buddha is not a garden gnome

Readily available in most garden centres, earthenware buddhas now sit alongside flamingos on sticks, tiki torches, miniature tin watering cans and families of gnomes. They are the hip orna- ment of choice for 'wellness' enthusiasts. And I get it, Buddha is a very relatable guy; he put on weight as he got older, his hair receded, what's not to like about him and his chilled-out teach- ings? His followers deserve a shout-out, too, for being so relaxed about Western people's penchant for sticking Buddha all over the place: in fountains and fish ponds, peering out from between the fiddle-leaf figs, perched way too close to the fire pit or barbeque. It's time to show a little more respect for the great man.

498
No armchairs in the bedroom

Unlike teenagers, who like to live, and grow mould cultures and possibly a little jazz cabbage, in their bedrooms, proper grown-ups don't spend a lot of time hanging out in their boudoir. It's really just a room for sleeping in. Which is why I find the trend for having a large comfy armchair or sofa in the bedroom rather odd. Even more odd is the fact that this chair is almost always angled to face the bed, suggesting it might be some kind of sex observation chair. By all means pop a standard chair in your room so you have something upon which to create a clothes mound instead of hanging things up, but get rid of the creepy sex-watcher armchair.

This rule is doubly important for anyone who believes in the spirit world. An armchair in the bedroom is like an open invitation for ghosts. One night you'll awaken to a familiar smack-smacking noise and look over to see the ghost of Nanna Jude sitting in the chair, sucking on a Werther's Original, waving her crochet at you.

499
Sleigh beds are for Santa and Mrs Claus

For the rest of us, they take up too much valuable real estate in the bedroom. Plus they're a pain in the arse to make every morning—reaching over, trying to tuck your sheets into the bottom end of the sleigh? Leave them for residents of the North Pole or anyone else who has elves to make the bed.

HOLIDAYS AND TRAVEL

One day the borders will reopen and we'll be able to travel again—until then, you can use this section to remind yourself of all the little things you don't miss about plane travel and holiday accommodation.

500
No irrelevant photos in the Airbnb listing

Photos of a jar of seashells in the bathroom—pointless. Same goes for that soft-focus snap of two wine glasses and a bottle of rosé on the kitchen bench. Especially if you don't plan to have said bottle of rosé sitting in the fridge for me to enjoy on arrival. Give me a close-up picture of the wi-fi password, so I know the place has internet access, a floor plan so I can see that there really are two bedrooms not just one bedroom and a cupboard with an air mattress, and maybe throw in a macro shot of the shower recess so I can check for mould. Do all that and I'll give you five stars just for your listing.

501
Provide useful amenities at your Airbnb

There appears to be some confusion over what guests actually require for an enjoyable holiday stay. Hosts seem to be under the impression that a guest's experience is enhanced by sticking giant words on the wall reminding them to DREAM, RELAX, FEEL or having decorative starfish in the bathroom to make it feel like you're under the sea when you're on the can. What guests would prefer is a sharp knife, a breadboard and a colander. Also, if it's an Airbnb, *supposedly* someone lives there, so why is the pantry completely empty? Would it kill you to have some salt and pepper in there? And if you really want to win friends and influence people, how about a little olive oil as well.

502
Two towels per person, minimum

This is not a rule; I think it's actually the law. And while we're on the topic of towels, a bath towel must be sizably bigger than a handtowel.

503
Call the council to remove hard rubbish, don't relocate it to your Airbnb

If you aren't using that hand-driven egg beater at home, there's every chance your guest won't use it either. Same goes for all those lightweight aluminium saucepans, rusty baking trays and that wonky frypan with the non-stick coating flaking off it in big black chunks.

504
White furniture is passive aggressive and unwelcoming

It says, *I dare you to sit on me.* It says, *You should expect to be charged an additional cleaning fee.* That is not, however, a free pass to go styling out your Airbnb with eye-assaulting bright-red furniture. No one can relax in a room that feels like a gaming den.

505
Respect the appliances in your hotel room

Other guests will have to use them at some stage. So don't iron black plastic bags. I can only assume this is what's happening because every time I go to use the iron in a hotel it's got black stuff melted all over it. And please don't use the kettle to boil soup.

506
Don't wear all of your luggage

Budget airlines keep the fare down by providing the bare minimum. A seat. And that's it. Anything else, like a bag or a biscuit or a bit of dignity, is going to cost you extra. That's why the canny travellers wear layer upon layer of clothing and stuff their pockets with phone chargers, shoes, iPads, bottled water, crushed up bags of McDonald's and other snacks, and then sew their jewels and valuables into the hems of their coats. Okay, maybe I made that last one up, but it's a fine line between wearing a few extra items to save on luggage costs and looking like you're escaping a fascist regime.

COMING OF AGE

A word about my generation

I am a member of Generation X, which includes anyone born between 1965 and 1980 or thereabouts. We are the generation who mistakenly believed we were going to redefine the modern world and fix everything, the ones who promised never to sell out. When Gen X poster boy Barack Obama took the reins in the United States, and a woman came to power in Australia, we thought, This is it, change starts now, time to clear up all those mistakes the Baby Boomers made. *Then, just like that (as Gen X golden girl Sarah Jessica Parker would say), we lost control. We ousted Julia Gillard from The Lodge, put a person of orange colour in charge of the White House and handed everything back to the conservative white men. What happened? Did we get lazy? Greedy? Did we become obsessed with stuff like home ownership and naming our kids after poets? Did we sell out? Did I just start writing like Carrie Bradshaw?*

I have separate rules for each generation, but I will start with Gen X. Not because I'm angry with us—I'm not—I'm just really, really disappointed.

_____→

GENERATION X

507
Accept that you have been rubbed down with vanishing cream

Lacking the wealth of the Baby Boomers and the youth of the Millennials, Generation X is currently the forgotten generation. Millennials, for example, don't even acknowledge that we exist as a separate demographic; they simply refer to anyone over forty as a 'Boomer'. Fair enough. We have been getting increasingly conservative about stuff. On the bright side, the Baby Boomers can't last forever and when they become extinct, hopefully it will be Gen X who inherit all that sweet, sweet Baby Boomer real estate. And then Millennials will *have* to acknowledge us, specifically for the purpose of hating us.

508
Not every band needs to get back together

By all means dust off those instruments and muck around in the garage or the backyard and talk about the good old days with your buds. But think very carefully before you drag your asses back onto a public stage and start charging your friends money to attend your reunion 'concert'. Respect that they might find it tough to watch your middle-aged paunch straining at those shirt buttons as you 'rock out' and sweat profusely under the hot lights. A sweaty young man on stage is one thing, but a sweaty fifty-something just makes everyone nervous and wonder if the venue has a defibrillator.

509
The time for giant underpants is now

Stop clinging to the vestiges of your come-hither youth and make the switch to big undies. The bigger the better. You want something comfortable enough to sit around in all day. You want to enjoy the secure feeling of pants that pull all the way up to your under-bosom. Forget about visible panty lines—your knickers will be riding so high everyone is going to mistake your VPL for a bra strap. Big underpants are like Jesus: you need to accept them into your life and wear them up close to your heart.

510
Don't use the phrase 'Okay Boomer'

This rejoinder is not for you, Gen X, it belongs to the youth. They came up with it, they're the ones who get to use it to dismiss anyone a minute older than them. Credit where it's due, it's a pretty good shutdown. Sure, it's overused and technic-ally inaccurate when they use it to scoff at Gen Xers. However, I will maintain my dignity and not get upset about that. There's nothing sadder than being 'okay boomered' and then desperately protesting 'But I'm Generation X!' All the young person hears is yet another old person making complaining noises.

Oh and also, 'nek minnit' finished a while back. You shouldn't say that either.

511
Leave the kooky glasses for Sir Elton

If you find your hand hovering above the oversized, coloured, 'statement' frames in the spectacle shop, remind yourself it's a slippery slope. You're only middle-aged at the moment, do you really want to fast-track yourself to old age? Because one minute you're putting big fun glasses on your face, the next you're heading out with bandaids on your face. Careful.

512
Put down the iPad stylus

I'm sure it works a treat but you look silly—like a four year old scrabbling away on a Magna Doodle, or the South Koreans in 2010 when they were using cocktail sausages to stab at their iPhones because their fingers wouldn't work in the cold weather. Come on, Gen X, don't be giving up on your body parts just yet; the time will come when you can sit around complaining about how things ache and don't work anymore but until then, no styluses.

513
Beware the unreliable sphincter

At some point during your late forties, your FWS (fart warning system) starts taking the occasional micro-nap. The majority of the time, you're totally in control; you sense trouble brewing below and you have time to either move away and release in a safe space, or clench and store it up for later. Sometimes, however, as you age, you get caught off guard. Your FWS goes down, and the first you know about it is when that pent-up air fires out of you like a gunshot and reverberates around the room or, indeed, Spotlight (if you're unlucky like me). The trick is knowing how to react when a surprise fart attack occurs. The best thing to do is to stand perfectly still. You need to freeze in position and catch the eye of someone nearby. Affect a look of mild disdain and raise an eyebrow at them. With any luck you'll have them thinking, *Oh my god, was that me?*

514
Don't trust 'facts' about vaccines that you find on Facebook

Of all the demographics, Gen X has fallen the hardest for Facebook, and it shows. Once we were the cool, 'we invented Nirvana and The Big Day Out' generation; now we're the vax-hesitant, 'I don't trust the science because I read something alarmist on Facebook' generation. Scientists and medical researchers do all the heavy lifting and experimenting so we don't have to. It seems the only mistake they make is publishing their findings in peer-reviewed journals rather than posting them on Facebook. Time to give real science a few more likes.

BABY BOOMERS

515
Start every story with 'Stop me if I've told you this already'

As an old person, you have lived a long life and no doubt have plenty of stories, so why not dig deep and roll out some new content occasionally? We're all happy to let you have the talking stick, we just want to hear something different.

516
You must be in the same room to converse

You cannot shout at someone who is in a different part of the house and expect them to hear you. Would somebody please tell my parents.

517
Let the young person operate the iPad

If you want to show a young person something on your iPad, hand it over and let them drive it. It's hard for the tech-savvy youth to watch Baby Boomers tapping all over the screen, swiping up and down with an absurd and unnecessary level of vigour. I swear my mother gets a full upper-body workout every time she uses her iPad. Shoulder reconstructions are going to be the new knee replacements if old people don't take the swiping down a notch.

518
Resist the urge to share your ancestry.com research

This is not to suggest you shouldn't enjoy a good old rummage through your family history. If you've got the time, why not get on that iPad you love so much and start searching through the past. Just be aware that no one, not even members of your own family, will be as interested in your findings as you are. Unless, of course, your ancestor was some kind of eighteenth-century 'pants man' who dipped his wick all over the village and eventually died of syphilis. Nothing captures an audience's attention like syphilis.

519
Don't be afraid to embellish your findings

If you must share your family history, then get creative with it. True doesn't always equate to interesting, and you should never let the facts get in the way of some good ancestry. I guarantee the program *Who Do You Think You Are?* embellishes all the time. No one would watch it if they kept 'uncovering' pedestrian things like Russell Crowe's great-great-aunt was a seamstress. Boo. I'm bored. I want to hear that his great-great-aunt lived as a man, Albert Nobbs–style, and went on to become a world champion bare-knuckle boxer (who eventually died of syphilis).

520
Men's ladder privileges expire at fifty-five

Unless you're a tradie, in which case, I'll spot you a few extra years. But for the rest of you, get down from there. Seriously fellas, it's not going to end well.

521
Don't take photos with your iPad

Nothing gives away your age faster than holding up a giant tablet in front of your face to take a picture. I'm well aware that your iPad has a camera, but just because you *can* take photos with it, doesn't mean you should.

522
Just,, checkyr TEXT before))) you spend it clapping hands, screaming face emoji

Baby Boomers still seem largely unaware of predictive text and the role it can play in rendering your texts indecipherable. You need to check that all the words make sense, watch out for random punctuation and review any emojis to make sure they're conveying the right emojion. It's weird to get a crying laughing face at the end of a text that says 'We had to take the dog to the vet.' Possibly you've got a bad case of 'fat finger' combined with 'can't find my glasses' and you keep hitting the wrong things by accident. Or maybe it's time to consider getting a stylus. Oh I'm kidding! Just proofread your work before you press send.

523
Don't send memes to Millennials

They saw it two years ago. Gen X, this goes for you too. Don't send memes to your Gen Z kids. The basic rule of thumb is that memes can be traded *up* to the generation above or *within* your own generation. Don't meme down.

524
Get to the good bit

As people get older, they begin to obsess over the really unimportant details of a story. Like what time it was and what day of the week it happened. 'So, Jean was at the golf club on Monday. Hang on ... was it Monday? No ... I don't think it was Monday, maybe it was Tuesday ... Actually, do you know what? I think it was Wednesday.' Oh for god's sake, you're not Craig David, it doesn't matter what day it happened. Get to the bit about Jean being struck by lightning as she teed off!

MILLENNIALS

I feel it's pointless laying down rules for Millennials. They'll just 'Okay Boomer' anything written here. But sometimes it can be cathartic to shout into the wind, so here goes.

525
Learn to cook

Signing up for Hello Fresh or Marley's Spoon or Bitch Be Cookin' Din Dins isn't really cooking. Stop kidding yourself, you're not *that* busy. Put a podcast on and make some pasta.

526
Turn up for work unless you're sick

A lot of Millennials don't seem to realise that if you want to take a day off work, you need to be sick—or at least pretending to be sick. Instead, they believe you have the right to skip work anytime it's inconvenient.

I know a Millennial who texted their boss to say they couldn't come in because the fence had fallen down and they were worried about their dog escaping. As a devoted dog owner who would never put my dogs' welfare at risk, I completely understand this dilemma. As a person who knows the rules, however, I can tell you there are countless solutions to this problem.

You could put the dog in the house and go to work.

If you don't trust the dog in the house, put the dog in the laundry and go to work. If you don't have a laundry, stick the dog in the bathroom and go to work. You could take the dog to a friend's house and go to work. Take the dog to your mum's house and go to work.

As I said, there are myriad solutions to this problem and pretty much all of them end with 'and go to work'.

527
If you do call in 'sick', stay off social media

Too sick to work? Then you're too sick to go to the beach. I'm not saying you can't go to the beach, I'm saying don't be foolish enough to post pictures of yourself at the beach. Show a modicum of intelligence.

528
Forget the eighties

If there is a decade of fashion that should be consigned to the rubbish bin rather than the recycling, it's the eighties. When you look back at movies from the sixties you think, *Ooh gee, don't they all look tidy!* Even looking back at the seventies you can still find plenty of positives: certain men really rocked those hip-hugging tight pants and large lapels, as did some ladies. However, eighties fashion did nothing for no one. No one was rocking it.

Take a movie like *Working Girl* from 1988, for example. Melanie Griffith played an ambitious young secretary keen to be taken seriously as a businesswoman, yet she was dressed like a portly Amish woman with shoulder pads?

That's what eighties fashion did, it made everyone look like stout middle-aged women. And there's absolutely nothing wrong with looking like a stout middle-aged woman, provided you are one. But we were teenagers and twenty-somethings. So could Millennials please stop trying to bring back this vile decade by referring to it as 'vintage'? It's very triggering. And you look dreadful, just like we did. You'll be sorry.

GENERATION Z

There's a lot to love about Generation Z. I love their faces, unravaged by time or surgery. I love that they decided to protest climate change by taking the day off school. What a simple and yet ingenious way to get more young people to turn up and support the cause. And may I say, you're going to need a lot more of that ingenuity if you're ever going to fix this mess of a planet we've gifted you. So Generation Z, I wish you all the best; here are a few rules I hope might be of help.

529
TikTok is not a job

It's been a tough time for Gen Z. Thanks to the pandemic, you've missed a lot of seminal moments in your school or university years. Graduations, formals, schoolies—they all got cancelled, but that doesn't mean you can't still aspire to greatness or at least do a little more with your life than make TikTok videos. Also, that platform is creepy; you do realise it actually spies on you and observes your expressions? TikTok is the modern-day equivalent of the dirty old perv hiding in the bushes watching you.

530
Don't eat your meals in the bedroom

The bedroom is for sleeping and, if you must, gaming. The kitchen and dining room are the eating chambers of the house and you should avail yourselves of these wonderful amenities. Don't hibernate in your bedroom surrounded by towers of dirty bowls and cups. Both you and the room need some fresh air, air that isn't heavy with the stench of your latest Uber Eats delivery. Parents need to play their part in this rule too—if you want to lure the kids out of their burrows, you need to promise not to badger them with questions like 'Did you only just wake up?!' or 'Aren't you supposed to go to work today?' or 'Have you filled out that form yet?' or 'How many people will be at the party?'

531
Be patient with old people who get your pronoun wrong

We're working on it, I promise.

532
Not everything is a toxic message

Sometimes your parents just say dumb stuff. So do you. Cut each other some slack.

533
Anyone sleeping over needs to come out and say hello

You are the generation that is in no rush to move out of home and who can blame you? Rent is expensive and house prices are laughable. Plus you have Gen X parents who are desperate to be seen as the 'cool parents'. They're not just Mum and Dad, they're your pal, your BFF, your bestie. And that is really working in your favour. Many teens now get given a double bed. Not only that, a lot of you are allowed to have sex in your bedroom. Some of the sensible/I'm-too-young-to-be-a-grandparent parents even put condoms in your drawers. It's a pretty sweet deal and nothing like the old days when teens had to clamber in and out of bedroom windows to avoid getting caught together. You need to show your appreciation for all these perks by offering your parents a crumb of congeniality in return. Whoever sleeps over in your bedroom must come out and say hello in the morning. It's potentially awkward, sure, but just tell your friend to pop some pants on (please) and come out to say hi. Trust me, it will make your parents' day.

534
Be discreet

During your 'sleepovers', keep the noise down. No sounds of enjoyment should escape the walls. That's the small price you pay for being allowed to do it at home. You must do it quietly. 'Cos you know what's even more awkward and uncomfortable than the thought of your parents 'doing it'? The thought of your kids doing it.

SPECIAL PANDEMIC TIMES SECTION
THE BASICS

In the beginning we tried to be positive. We waxed on about getting to know our neighbours (mostly because we were desperate to talk to anyone who didn't live inside our own four walls) and we hashtag glad-gamed about the lack of traffic on the roads and not having to do the daily commute. Working mothers revelled in a sense of schadenfreude as they listened to men complain about how hard it is to work from home with the kids running around. And we turned every day into Christmas Day, selflessly keeping Australia Post afloat as Postman Santa worked around the clock to deliver all those late-night, wine-fuelled

online purchases we made with PayPal (or as I like to call it, 'pretend click money').

I tried to take comfort in the little things, like getting to see how messy other people's houses were, courtesy of Zoom. I'd always assumed my pigsty of a home was the outlier, but it turns out loads of people are untidy. It made me feel good, but also made me wonder why these people didn't do what I do and keep one small corner of the house tidy for Zoom meetings.

In the beginning, I never imagined I'd need to write a bunch of rules for a pandemic but now, almost two years into this thing, with everyone thinking, 'Jesus Christ, when will it END?!' I see that I have no choice. It's time to pivot and apply my special rule-making gift to this global crisis.

535
Stop chowing down on endangered species

Whether you believe Covid-19 started in a bat, a lab, Bill Gates' secret lair or a weird scaly animal at a wet market in Wuhan, this rule shouldn't be exclusive to pandemic times. Note, please: I am not having a stab at China here—I have no beef with China. Nor do many of our cattle producers at the moment, apparently. I'm just suggesting we could all lay off eating exotic and endangered species. Especially if the only reason you're doing it is because you think their ground-up horns or toenails will give you a magical erection. I know it's hard to believe but some things are slightly more important than your penis, guys.

536
Don't hoard like an idiot

Not once, in any state, at any time, have the supermarkets closed. There has never been an actual shortage of anything. The only reason anyone has been forced to go without pasta or mince or toilet paper is because panic buyers stripped the shelves. I imagine doomsday preppers around the world watched footage of those frenzied supermarket shoppers in disbelief. Preppers know better than to run blindly into a store and start grabbing mindlessly at whatever's in front of them. (They also know that once a lockdown has been called, it's too late, you've missed the boat.) So if you really must hoard, do it like a pro: hoard hard and hoard early. Obviously you want to avoid anything that needs refrigeration 'cos you don't want to drain your 'genny' (that's prepper talk for generator). You need to grab packet soups, Spam, canned fish or cat food (it's the same thing), powdered milk and, I would also suggest, some sheets of nori. Seaweed contains a lot of essential vitamins and minerals and could potentially double as toilet paper in an emergency.

537
No fighting in the supermarket aisles

Given that there will always be people who ignore the no-hoarding rule, it's up to the rest of us to lead by example. Walk away from a shouting match or physical scrap in the supermarket. Reassure yourself that, as a species, humans have survived for hundreds of thousands of years. We're bipedal cockroaches. Look at North Korea: they haven't had food for decades, and while you might not fancy a bowl of stick and gravel soup, it does seem to be sustaining a large percentage of the North Korean population.

As for brawling over toilet paper, have you lost your mind, man? Maintain your dignity, use your oversized human brain and come up with a solution. How about washing your bumhole? Lots of men out there for whom that wouldn't be a bad idea, toilet paper shortage or not. Sluicing out your bot might be slightly inconvenient but I'm making the point that there is always an alternative to punching on with someone in Woolworths. After all, it's only a pandemic, not the zombie apocalypse.*

* *FYI, when the zombies come, all bets are off. I'm shooting you in the head and prising the toilet paper out of your cold dead hands.*

538
Dance like nobody's watching, shop like somebody's filming

If you think you might struggle to remember the rule about not fighting in supermarkets, then perhaps this will help you keep yourself nice—always assume that someone, somewhere is filming you, which means the minute you do anything stupid you will be publicly shamed by every news outlet around the world. None of the networks care anymore about broadcast quality. They'll take out-of-focus, jerky iPhone footage any day, provided it shows members of the public screaming and beating one another with value packs of pasta.

539
Support your local bakery

The bakery is considered an essential service. It's open. I know you've been on the internet and learnt how to make sourdough. I know your loaf was made with love (tonnes of it, if the weight of the loaf is anything to go by) and I know everyone in the house took turns feeding 'the mother'. Together you created a loaf that made you feel more connected as a family. And I'm sure that with half a pound of butter slathered on every slice, that loaf is perfectly edible. You had a go and good on you, but that's enough now. It's time to admit that lockdowns are hard enough and you shouldn't punish yourself with dense bricks of damp dough. Get some properly delicious bread from the bakery.

540
Before you 'pivot' your business to produce hand sanitiser, make sure you have a decent recipe

After living with Covid-19 for this long, many of us are now hand-sanitiser connoisseurs. In the beginning we really appreciated the many small businesses who stepped up to help meet demand and manufacture much-needed hand sanitiser. But with supply now well under control, it feels like a good time to finesse your formula if you plan to stay in the sanitiser game. You're aiming for something that doesn't sting like pure alcohol, doesn't smell like paint stripper or a trough lolly, and doesn't run all over your hands like water. Oh, and thank you for your service.

541
Don't make a TV show about life in lockdown

No one wants to watch that. If you're going to spend money on TV production, make something that helps us forget about the pandemic. We've got the news if we want to be depressed.

542
Scan the QR code and step aside to fill out the rest

And, yes, I'm afraid I'm looking at you, old people. God bless you for checking in, just please be aware of the pile-up happening behind you.

SHOP TALK

CONSUMERS

543
No one needs special cheese cutlery

Cheese is fairly easy to cut, as evidenced by the late-night infomercials that advertise items like the 'Miracle Knife' or the 'Wonder Blade'. They never use a wheel of cheese in these demonstrations. The shouty presenter is always carving through things like tin cans and old leather shoes. But a chunk o' cheddar? Nup. Because *any* knife will cut cheese. In fact, I'm pretty confident any spoon will cut cheese. I've even used a wooden chopstick to cut cheese; it's not ideal but it works fine. My point is, your kitchen drawer overfloweth with cheese-cutting implements, you do not need to buy a special miniature cheese cleaver. Unless, of course, you are a mouse and you have some serial killing to do.

544
Always buy a backup avocado

The avocado is a high-risk purchase, so if your meal is avocado-dependent you don't want to bet the house on one single fruit. And if you're a straight man who has been sent to get the groceries, I suggest you buy at least three.

545
Avoid single-use appliances

Much like specific cutlery for cheese, there are plenty of items you and your kitchen can live without. Even if you have room in your 'butler's pantry', why not save the space, save your money and invest in an actual butler to live in there instead. I guarantee you already have everything you need in your kitchen to prepare delicious food. Show me your rice cooker, I will show you my saucepan with a well-fitting lid; show me your milkshake-maker, I will show you my blender; show me your elaborate countertop coffee-maker, I will show you my beardy guy with the man bun down at the local cafe.

But, just in case you've been watching too many cooking shows and are feeling tempted, here is a detailed list of things you don't need.

SOUS VIDE MACHINE
I'm not a French speaker but I believe *sous vide* translates to 'over-rated slow-boiled meat' and the good news is, you don't need a special machine to make that magic happen. Just pop your steak into a ziplock bag, boil for forty minutes and voila! You're halfway to that classic French bistro dish, Warm Grey Meat & Frites. Enjoy.

FOOD DEHYDRATOR
Don't be tempted by this contraption, mostly because if you look around your kitchen you'll see you already have one. It's

called an oven. Stick it on low and start drying out all the food you need for that trip to space you must be planning. Why else would you be dehydrating food?

AIRFRYER

Due to its size, the airfryer is often mistaken for a small caravan, and you might actually find yourself needing to park it out on the street for the 364 days of the year you're not using it. The enjoyable paradox of this huge appliance is its relatively tiny cooking basket, which holds a mere handful of chips. If you're that worried about cooking with too much oil, try putting less oil on your food before cooking it.

ICE CREAM MAKER

You really don't have to make everything 'from scratch'. Modern life is not a self-sufficiency competition and there's no actual survivalist value in making your own ice cream. Plant a few herbs instead.

EGG POACHER

None of them work. None. If you need a foolproof way to poach an egg, I refer you to season one, episode one, of the program *Amy Schumer Learns to Cook*. Even my nephew has mastered this method to perfectly poach eggs for himself every morning.

RETAILERS

546
Don't misdirect the buying public

Recently I sat myself down in a very swanky-looking cocktail bar and looked up at the unfamiliar list of cocktails on the wall, things like Buzz Cut, Hot Towel Shave and Lemon Myrtle Pomade. Fortunately I realised I was in a barber shop before I ordered a delicious sounding Tidy Beard Sculpt. Given the huge hit retail has taken during the pandemic, now seems like a good time to remind vendors of the need to be clear about the goods and services on offer. Besides the barber shop/wine bar confusion, I've noticed that many real estate agencies are now fitting themselves out like cafes. I've also mistaken the post office for a two-dollar shop, Aldi for a rubbish tip and a tattoo parlour for a jewellery store (that necklace is never coming off).

547
Put the cash registers at the front, Kmart

Kmart moved their registers to the middle of the store, claiming it was to keep the entrances clear and allow for easy coming and going. But shoppers aren't stupid. We know why they did it. For the same reason supermarkets put the milk at the back of the store—so that you're forced to walk past umpteen other tempting items on the way. Kmart think they have created a fun treasure-hunt experience. Their hope is that as you search for the tills 'buried' in the middle of the store, you will pass loads of other precious treasure and be tempted to add it to your cart. But the problem is, Kmart, you don't sell treasure, you sell landfill.

548
Not everything needs to be 'monetised'

It's okay to keep your hobby as something you enjoy doing in your free time. Don't feel pressured by overly supportive friends and family who say things like, 'Oh my god, these pupcakes are amazing, my dog loves them, you should totally go on Shark Tank, you could make a fortune.' You could . . . but you probably won't and there's every chance you'll stop enjoying making marrow muffins for mutts once you have to worry about spreadsheets and inventory and distribution and all those other boring business things. Also, let's be honest, not everything needs to be scaled up. Some things were meant to be sold only at markets. Things like jewellery made from forks, hemp-based baby swaddles, flavoured honey that never tastes any different to regular honey, tree-stump furniture and upcycled shopping bag aprons. And if you're a scented candlemaker, you definitely want to keep that small-scale and recreational. The market is awash with scented candles, so much so that if the global wax mines dried up tomorrow, we would still have enough candles for everyone, forever.

CAFES

549
Remove the lettuce before toasting the sandwich

I understand it's fast and convenient to have your sandwiches prepped and waiting in the glass cabinet and that it's inconvenient to take the lettuce off, then toast the sandwich, then put the lettuce back on, but no one wants a chicken and hot lettuce sandwich. Full disclosure, my mother asked me to include this rule.

550
Baristas must be able to talk and froth simultaneously

No one minds a chatty barista, provided they are able to talk and make the coffee at the same time. But when you are standing at the back of a long line and the barista keeps taking his foot off the frothing gas in order to chitty chat, that's when the customers start getting antsy. Talk and froth, guys, talk and froth.

551
Three takeaway coffees max per customer

During peak periods, cafes should be allowed to put up a sign that limits customers to two or three takeaway coffees. We've all been on a tight schedule, walked past the cafe, seen a couple of people queuing and thought, *Yep, I've got time, I'll make it* and joined the end of the line. Only to have some clown in front of you get to the counter and start rattling off a coffee order for the entire office, punctuating said order with, 'Oh and do you do milkshakes by any chance?'

552
Social distance your diners

This is not about venue capacity during a pandemic; this pertains to those waiters who insist on seating you right on top of other diners when there are still plenty of free tables elsewhere in the restaurant. The oft-volunteered excuse of 'I'm sorry, I have to sit you in my section' is baloney. If there is genuinely such a strict demarcation of sections, then sit me in someone else's section and send that section-master over to take my order. Or, if there's no one on shift yet to service that section, make like a politician and cross the floor yourself.

553
Put some thought into the vegetarian option

Vegetarians appreciate it when you have an option for them; they are not ungracious people. But there is not a vegetarian in the world who needs to eat another stuffed mushroom, stuffed capsicum, or anything that relies on huge chunks of cold, wet pumpkin. And for the love of god, stop calling slabs of vegetables set into a solid block of egg a 'fritatta'—that's not a fritatta, it's an 'egg-wodge' and no one likes it.

554
No naked leaves

Putting a bunch of dry greenery on the side of a plate is tantamount to food waste. You may as well throw it straight in the bin. But if you toss those leaves in a decent amount of dressing, then we'll have a go at them.

555
Hang up before you approach the counter

All shops and cafes should be allowed to have a sign on the door that clearly states:

FOR HEALTH AND SAFETY REASONS,
WE CANNOT SERVE YOU WHILE YOU ARE ON THE PHONE

Because when you walk in yammering away on your phone, pause momentarily to bark out a coffee order then go right back to your call, it takes a lot of restraint for the person behind the counter not to reach out, snatch that phone and whack you over the head with it. So, for your own safety, please get off the phone and engage in a courteous and human-like manner with the shopkeep. And don't excuse yourself by saying that the call is important. if it was that important, you wouldn't be stopping to get a coffee.

CLEAR COMMUNICATION

TEXTING AND EMAILING

556
No one really believes 'OMG! I just saw this msg now for some reason!'

It's like when someone doesn't reply to your email for weeks then sends a missive headed 'OMG I just found your email in my junk folder.' Maybe that's true, or maybe you're a liar liar, pants on fire, in which case it's much better to start your text or email with a simple 'Sorry I've taken so long to reply.' No need to elaborate, just offer an apology, straight up with no qualifier. The exception to this rule is if the email saying 'I just found this in my junk folder' comes from me, in which case I swear it's true.

557
Abbreviations in texts should be easy to decipher

Occasionally you have to concede that sending a WTF or an OMG is convenient—it may not be your personal style, but everyone understands the impulse to send them. Other abbreviations, however, will simply never catch on. When has 'tks' ever saved anyone time? It's not immediately obvious it means 'thanks', so all it does is momentarily confuse the reader. It really would be quicker to just tap out the word 'thanks'; it's not a long word and I'll tk you not to waste my time in future.

558
Don't avoid the grieving

As a general rule, it's perfectly fine to send a tasteful text when someone dies. Not to the dead person (obviously) but to the family and friends. Don't hand-wring over the idea that you might 'interrupt the grieving process' or that you didn't know the family well enough to send a text. And definitely don't *not* send a text because you're worried about saying the wrong thing. All of these things are about you. People like to know you're thinking about them, so text them and let them know, just don't expect a reply; recognise that the grief text is a one-way exchange.

Important caveat for anyone over sixty—when signing off on a text to a grieving person, remember LOL does not stand for lots of love.

559
e-cards are meaningless

They say either, 'I forgot' or 'I didn't care enough to get you an actual card but I still want the points for sending one'. I would much rather you just sent me a three-word email that said, 'Happy birthday, mate!' Or one of those text messages that does something explosive when you open it up: fireworks go off, balloons float up, confetti rains down or, the best one, lasers crisscross the screen—that one actually makes noise and buzzes in your hand. It's a multi-sensory experience. I get such a childish kick out of receiving them, I often play them over and over. If you don't know what I'm talking about, ask a young person to send you one; they're quite magical.

560
Don't weaponise your birthday

After a certain age, it really doesn't matter if people forget your birthday. Everyone's busy. And no one is forgetting your birthday to spite you. One of my mother's main jobs in our family is to text everyone else a reminder that someone's birthday is coming up so no one feels forgotten. This year I decided to cut out the middle man and send the reminder to my siblings myself. As soon as I woke up, I texted, 'Hi guys, it's my birthday today, don't forget to send me a text saying *Happy Birthday*.' It was a big success. We've agreed this is the way forward.

KIDS PARTY INVITATIONS

561
Be specific, leave nothing open to interpretation

In days of yore (well, back in the seventies) my mother used to drop me at my friends' birthday parties by slowing the car down, shouting, 'Tuck and roll!' then pushing me out the door. I'd barely be through the front gate before she was out of sight and already enjoying her child-free afternoon.

Not so these days. Parents tend to stick around. So not only do you have to entertain the kids, you also have to entertain the parents. Which can be a lot of work, especially if you don't really know these parents. I understand that when kids are very young, you might want other parents to stay and help wrangle a house full of preschoolers hopped up on sugar and party vibes. But once the kids can competently toilet themselves and articulate things like 'Joshua has fallen off the trampoline and now his leg looks weird', lingering parents can be a real drag. To avoid any confusion, I suggest making it clear on the invitation, much like you would with a dress code. Simply state: 'This is a Drop & Go event. Drop at 2 pm. Go. Pick up at 5 pm.' Do not, under any circumstances, forget to state the pick-up time.

LANGUAGE

I understand English is a living language but that doesn't mean we shouldn't be able to kill things off occasionally.

562
You can't verse people

You can play against or versus a person. But to say 'I'm versing someone' sounds as if you're aggressively reciting poetry at them.

563
Medal is not a verb

It's time to return to 'winning medals' at the Olympics rather than 'medalling'. Medalling makes it sound like you're talking about a pesky kid who snuck into the athletes' village and mixed up the urine samples. Plus, we all know that if an athlete has medalled it's just code for 'didn't win gold'. Same goes for podium. No one is podiuming. Or has podiumed. Or will be podiuming. Can you not hear how ridiculous it sounds?

564
Talk 'about it' not 'to it'

This recent affectation of speaking 'to' things rather than about things has really taken off.

'Hmm, you raise an interesting point about language, can you speak *to* that some more?'

I can only assume people think it makes them sound intellec-
tual when, in reality, it makes them sound like someone who's
watched too many Oprah interviews.

565
Stop devaluing words

'Absolutely' is used so often in place of the word 'yes' that
it has little meaning anymore as a word that adds emphasis.
Youthful call centre operators also like to abuse adjectives such
as 'amazing' and 'fantastic', using them to punctuate the most
pedestrian exchanges:

'Can I start with your name?'

'Sam.'

'Amazing. And is this the phone number you're calling about?'

'Yep.'

'Faaantastic.'

Hmm, is it? I would argue that being able to cite things like your
own name, address and phone number is completely unremark-
able unless you're recovering from some kind of *Memento*-style
traumatic memory loss.

Similarly, we've managed to wreck the words 'awesome' and
'epic'. They both now mean little more than 'okay'.

'I'll pick up some cat food on my way home.'

'Awesome, that would be epic.'

Hardly. Even my cat, who loves food more than life itself, would
tell you that response is disproportionate. At best it deserves a
thumbs up and a thankyou.

566
Optics schmoptics

This is really the same as the above, with people thinking they sound more intelligent if they say 'The optics aren't good on that' rather than 'Ooh gee, that looks bad'. And while we're at it, referring to a lamp as 'a piece' and the room as 'the space' just makes you sound up yourself.

567
Four things you shouldn't say about yourself

I'm a smart person.
I'm very creative.
I'm really good in bed.
I'm such an empath.

Rest assured it's okay to *think* all of these things about yourself, and it's perfectly fine for other people to say these things about you. But when you say them yourself, unfortunately all anyone hears is 'I'm a bit of a dick.'

568
Four things you shouldn't say to try to sound interesting

I'm a clean freak.
I'm thinking about quitting sugar.
I'm a full-on foodie.
I'm passionate about event management.

Again, there is nothing wrong with doing or being any of these things, just don't mistake them for conversation starters.

569
Four things you shouldn't ask a teenager

What subjects are you doing?
Who was at the party?
Why don't you open the blinds?
Is there a funny smell in here?

570
Don't use the word 'hubby'

I know it's quick and easy but for some reason 'hubby' always conjures up an image of a chubby man hiding in a cupboard, rather than the grown man who is your husband.

571
Curb your Americanisms

I don't mind the occasional Americanism—for example, anaesthesiologist looks hard but is actually easier to say than anaesthetist. Others, however, are just plain grating, especially when they come out of children's mouths. I think teachers should put up posters around our classrooms to remind kids that in this country we say:

Bum not butt
Poo not poop
Lollies not candy
My fault not my bad

And as for 'dang it'—why are we letting Australian kids talk like hillbillies? I think I'd almost prefer they said 'f**k it'. Almost. Cookie vs biscuit is mildly controversial. I acknowledge that biscuit is what we say here in Australia; however, I will accept cookie when preceded by 'homemade chocolate chip' or indeed 'Oreo'. Conversely, Anzac can only be followed by biscuit. In fact, I believe that saying 'Anzac cookie' could see you arrested for treason.

572
Ass is funny, arse is harsh

Many readers might have expected ass and arse to be included in the rule about curbing Americanisms. However, this is a tricky one for me. I often use 'ass' in my writing because I think it sounds amusing. And, in my mind, ass is also less aggressive than arse. 'Move your fat ass.' That's funny. 'Move your fat arse.' You just crossed a line, that's highly offensive. But here's the twist: I would never call someone an 'asshole'—it feels weak and ineffectual. If you're annoyed with someone to the point of insulting them, then you want a word with a bit of punch. And that's arsehole. Always arsehole. It's a good, strong word. Basically, what I've just admitted is that all my rules are completely arbitrary, subjective nonsense. Enjoy.

SPECIAL PANDEMIC TIMES SECTION
MASKS

Trigger warning:

Please skip the next few pages if the idea of
wearing a mask makes you apoplectic and inclined
to send me death threats. I'm here to entertain,
not to enrage. You've been warned, so either move
on or climb aboard my mask-wearing train!

573
Wear a mask

I'm a big believer in science and this one's been proven time and time again by an experiment that even I can understand. It's quite literally, 'Okay everyone, look how far spit droplets go *without* a mask on. Now look how far they go *with* a mask on.' Try it at home if you don't believe me. First spit with a mask off, then spit again with a mask on. The results will amaze you.

574
Brush your teeth before putting your mask on

One of the worst things about wearing a mask is being confronted with the occasional reality of your own bad breath. Brushing before fitting your mask can stop you going into a daily spiral of 'Oh my god, is this acrid stench what I've been breathing on people my entire life? How do I still have any friends?' You might want to carry mints for when brushing is not an option but avoid extra-strong mints if you wear glasses, 'cos the fumes that get funnelled up from those suckers are enough to melt your eyeballs.

575
Masks go over mouths and noses

People who wear their mask at half-mast with their nose hanging out over the top don't seem to understand the function of the mask, or indeed the nose. The mask is there to stop droplets and germs; the nose is there to help you breathe and produce snot. In other words, the core business of the nose is to make and dispense droplets and germs. I don't think anyone should be fined for incorrect mask wearing, instead I think they should be forced to wear an exemption in the form of a T-shirt that says I'M A MOUTH-BREATHER.

576
Don't feel obliged to have fun with masks

A standard paper mask is fine. It's enough that you wear a mask and tolerate it, no one expects you to enjoy it or make it a fun fashion statement.

577
Focus on the positives

In summer, wearing a mask can be stifling, but in winter it does quite a nice job of keeping your face warm, kind of like a balaclava without the terrorist overtones. Masks also make close-talkers and people with bad breath a lot more bearable. As for bank robbers? Why on earth aren't they all out robbing themselves stupid? Gone are the signs that say, *Remove your face covering before entering the bank.* These days you're not allowed in the bank *without* covering your face. So stop sitting around complaining about the restrictions and get out there, you clowns, it's salad days for bank robbers! (Just be aware that depending on lock-down laws, you might need to restrict your robbing to within a five to ten kilometre radius of your hideout.)

578
Don't argue with retail staff about
your right not to wear a mask

Take it up with the government. Or take it to the streets and protest about your right to spread Covid, whatever you need to do in order to 'feel heard'. And if you're running out of ways to demonstrate that the rules don't apply to you—if punching horses and setting off flares in the CBD isn't sending your message strongly enough—then might I suggest you start burning my books? I'd be so touched, and I really think it would make your point about not believing in rules.

Just don't be a coward and make your stand by shouting at some poor person in a shop or a cafe, someone who neither makes the rules nor has any power to change the rules. Anti-maskers love to bellow about rights but what about the rights of the person behind the counter? Surely they have the right not to be abused in their own workplace?

579
Show your exemption letter politely

I know some people have legitimate grounds for not wearing a mask and it must get boring being asked to show your exemption letter all the time, but hey, it's boring for a fisherman to be asked if they're 'catching any today' or a cab driver to be asked 'You just starting or finishing?' or breakfast radio presenters to be asked 'What time do you have to get up in the morning?' But they all still manage to respond politely. Waving your exemption aggressively in somebody's face makes it difficult to read and also creates suspicion. Hang on, is that a genuine exemption you're flapping or is it just something you printed off the web? Something that says, 'I am a sovereign citizen, I have the right not to wear a mask according to subsection (b) of law 251 of Internet-Land.'

FOOD STUFF

EATING

580
Never make eye contact with someone while eating a banana

After about the age of twelve, you need to be mindful of your banana consumption. What was once a fun fruit for monkeys and children suddenly becomes an undignified, innuendo-laden snack. Eat them in public if you must but keep your eyes cast downwards.

581
No eating on the phone

Be aware that people usually take a phone call by holding the phone to their ear. So if you're chewing while talking to someone on the phone, the sound of your smack-smackery is going directly into their earhole. It's like you've put your mouth right onto their ear and started masticating. It's offensive.

582
Bring your food up to your mouth, don't take your face down to your plate

Food is always exciting when it arrives at the table but it's important to remember, we're not livestock in a barn. Keep your head up, don't lower it down to the trough and start snuffling.

583
If your food is too hot, stop eating it

We've all seen idiots do it. And we've all been the idiot who's done it, whether it's tucking into a bowl of visibly steaming risotto or a pizza straight out of the oven covered in molten lava-like cheese. You take a bite and instantly know you've made a mistake. You wave your hand up and down in front of your open mouth, fanning the food and huffing out words of warning to everyone at the table: 'Ahhh, haht, haht, haht, 's too haht!' Then you start chewing at your food like a ventriloquist dummy laughing. Eventually you swallow it and say again, for anyone at the table who might have missed your performance, 'Oh my god, that is too hot!' Then what happens? You go straight back in and take another bite. For the love of god, stop. Give it a minute to cool down. Let's earn our place at the top of the food chain.

584
No crunching at the cinema

After more than a year of not being able to go to the movies, cinemas briefly opened again and I couldn't wait to get back into a dark room with strangers to see a film on the big screen. I steeled myself, ready to cope with the popcorn stench, but I'd forgotten about the potato chips. First comes the relentless rustling as the dirty chip-eater takes an eternity to open the bag and then comes the infernal surround-sound crunching. My god, it's so loud, shut up, people! Rip the bag open quickly and then please, for the love of god, suck your chips.

COOKING

585
Spiralisers are not magic wands

They cannot turn vegetables into pasta. Pasta is comforting. Zucchini 'noodles' and carrot 'ribbons' are good for you and they're pretty to look at but they're never going to trip your satisfaction trigger like pasta.

586
Cauliflower is not rice

It's not a pizza base either, despite what followers of the keto diet would have you believe. For the record, I like cauliflower. I find it quite tasty. Small florets tossed in olive oil, a few chilli flakes and roasted in the oven then lightly salted would be my preparation of choice if anyone's interested. I also don't mind finely grated cauliflower, it's perfectly nice. But it's not rice. How do I know? 'Cos rice isn't just nice, it's bloody delicious.

587
Don't microwave leftover pizza

I don't own a microwave because I'm concerned about radio-active 5G waves melting my synapses. Oh I'm kidding! I'm not frightened of microwaves but I do think you get a much better result reheating leftover pizza in a frying pan. Tiny bit of oil in the bottom of the frying pan, put the slices in the pan and then cover with a lid for a couple of minutes. Bottom fries up nice and crispy, while the lid creates steam and makes the cheese all soft and gooey again. Alright, I admit it, this one isn't really a rule—it's a HACK, and it's my special gift to you.

588
Go easy on the food fusion

Despite what you see on *MasterChef*, everything is not suddenly improved or made 'next level' by whacking it in a taco or a bao, or by adding a side of kimchi. Sure, kimchi is good for you and I know it's an integral part of Korean cuisine, but isn't it also just spicy wet cabbage?

589
A medjool date is not a dessert

Nor is a cup of green tea a 'great substitute' for that sweet biscuit or cake you normally have for afternoon tea. Drink as much green tea as you like, just don't try to pass it off as anything but grassy water.

590
Just say no to dukkah

It sounds delicious on paper; a mixture of nuts and seeds and spices, it looks exotic and smells exciting. Yet when you dip your bread in the oil and the dukkah, then take a bite, invariably the first thing you think is, 'Ooh, dust and gravel, num num!'

A word about the Christmas menu

Everyone thinks there are a lot of rules about what to serve up at Christmas time. Wrong.

Let's start with the turkey. Turkey is not compulsory. Some of us don't have an oven big enough to cook one, or a family big enough to eat one. And some of us think turkey is completely overrated and tasteless, no matter how much you brine it, baste it or stuff its hole with sausage mince and chestnuts. You also shouldn't feel obliged to spend hours queuing at the fish market on Christmas Eve to buy prawns. I know we're in Australia and we love waving our sunshine and fresh seafood platters in English people's faces during the festive season but the pressure to mortgage your house to pay for overpriced Christmas prawns is too much.

And can we all please calm down about the ham? I think the whole ham thing is a beat-up created by butchers. They put signs *everywhere saying* Don't forget to order your Christmas ham *and everyone falls for it, thinking,* Yes, that's right, we need an entire ham. *Ordinarily a dozen slices from the deli would suffice, but at Christmas time, suddenly we become Henry the Eighth and require an entire haunch of pig for our banqueting table.*

So the only rule is to cook whatever you and your family like to eat. Obviously make sure potatoes are included in some form, be it roasted, mashed, chipped or saladed. No need to be the potato grinch and ruin Christmas for everyone.

——————————————————→

RECIPE WEBSITES

591
Cakes require more than two ingredients

If you don't have time to bake a cake that's absolutely fine, but don't kid yourself that you can cheat the system by using a two-ingredient recipe 'hack'! The internet would have you believe you can make a delicious cake from a tin of pineapple and a cup of flour. But that's fake news. You don't get a cake, you get a rubbery lump of pineapple-flavoured wallpaper paste. You'd be better off just eating the tin of pineapple.

592
Enough with things in mugs and cobs

I want to eat my cake from a plate not a mug. I'm not an animal. And I see no reason to cook anything in one of those round white loaves of bread, otherwise known as 'a cob'. I've no objection to the cob loaf or to serving a cob loaf *with* your meal, but what is this obsession websites have with inserting the meal into the cob itself? I don't want my lasagne in a cob or beef stroganoff in a cob and I definitely don't want chicken korma in a cob. The only thing that should be served in a cob is French onion dip at a seventies party.

593
No more cheesecake recipes

Every possible iteration of a cheesecake already exists. There is nothing new you can do with it; everything's been covered. The base can be made from biscuit or breakfast cereal or gluten-free kitty litter, or it can be baseless; the filling can be cream cheese or ricotta or yoghurt or sour cream or all of the above with absolutely anything folded through it from Mars Bars to miso soup. Everything's been done, and the bottom line is, you can't go past a good baked cheesecake anyway. So everyone focus on mastering that and please stop taking up space on the web with 'new' cheesecake suggestions, there's almost no room for porn anymore.

594
Don't believe the hype about red velvet cake

Red velvet cake tricks me every time. It looks and sounds other-worldly, like a cake made in heaven. And yet it tastes like . . . nobody's really sure? The best I can describe it is, a half-strength chocolate cake, with red in it?

THE GREAT OUTDOORS

595
Stick to sandwiches at a picnic

Once a simple, pleasant, outdoor lunch on a rug, the picnic has somehow morphed into a complicated ordeal of platters and salads and expensive, oily comestibles from delis that leak all over everything else in your bag. A picnic is far more enjoyable when you're not forced to wrestle with cutlery or balance a plate on your lap or worry about that ticking salmonella time bomb that comes in the form of a greasy barbeque chicken. Keep it manageable and stick to hand-held, dripless food like old-school sandwiches (cut into triangles) and a thermos of sweet tea. It's important to leave people with one hand free to grab at the hat that's threatening to fly off their head or to remove the hair that keeps blowing into their mouth. Maybe have some biscuits or cupcakes or even fruit (apologies to my sister) for afters, but no elaborate cakes or anything that needs 'plating up'.

* *Obviously this is a rule for white people. I don't pretend to speak for other cultures. If you've got a nonna or a yaya etc. you can disregard this rule and enjoy your arancini or your dolmades, or even your whole roasted lamb on a spit. Those old dames are like one-woman catering trucks; the ease with which they can distribute food to the masses is extraordinary. They make Jesus and his 'fish sandwiches for 5000' look like an amateur.*

THE ART OF ENTERTAINMENT

PODCASTS

Everyone's got a podcast these days; I am no exception. I make one and I enjoy many. Unlike film or television or theatre, the podcast is lean, easy to produce and quick to turn around, which makes it the ideal piece of content for a pandemic. Podcasters are like the preppers of showbiz, sitting in their well-equipped bunkers, ready to go at a moment's notice. So praise be to the podcast, it's a great thing. Now let's keep it great with a few simple rules.

596
Have an idea

Many people can witter on about nothing but only some people can make those witterings interesting. Unfortunately, the few who *can* seem to have inspired the many who can't. I'm not saying you shouldn't do a podcast—by all means, get a microphone and get involved—just make sure you have a plan, something a little more detailed than 'I'm going to press record and start riffing.' Riffing is fine, provided you have an objective and an exit strategy.

597
One hour is ample

Any more than that and it's not really entertainment; it's you enjoying the sound of your own voice and/or exposing your own loneliness and desperate need to talk at people.

598
Just start

No need for long preambles or meandering apologies about why a new 'ep didn't drop' last week. Your listener gets it, and my guess is they also have many other podcasts in their library, so if you have to skip a week, I reckon they'll be okay; they have plenty of other content to fill the giant void your missing podcast has left.

599
Know who the murderer is before
releasing your cold case podcast

Most fans of true crime podcasts would be familiar with that uneasy feeling you get around week four or five when you start to suspect that a podcast is going nowhere. It's no longer moving forward but rather seems to be following a lot of tangents with no real substance. That's about the same time you google the case and realise you've been suckered and the crime remains unsolved. Keeping the tension alive by withholding information is all well and good—provided you actually *have* that information up your sleeve and plan to do a big Scooby Doo-style reveal in the final episode: 'And guess what, listener, turns out it was the caretaker, Mr Wickles, all along!' You're making a podcast, not a French film; please have an ending.

600
Not everyone can be Dax Shepard/Wil Anderson

If you are a well-loved celebrity or comedian, you might want to think carefully before starting your own podcast where you interview other celebrities and comedians. The celebrity-host-interviewing-celebrity-guest genre really started to eat itself during the pandemic. Maybe you're better off staying as that celeb who pops up occasionally as a really entertaining guest on other people's podcasts. Believe it or not, a lot of celebs are actually much better guests than they are hosts. Good hosts are happy to let their guests do some of the talking.

601
Podcasts should be off limits as sources of content for 'news' websites

One of the best things about podcasts when they first hit the scene was the fact that guests were so much more relaxed and prepared to speak freely. People said all sorts of things they'd never say during a regular press interview. It felt like the podcast was the black market of inside information. But then the tabloids started trawling the podcasts for content and now guests are starting to be a little more wary about what they say. Stop ruining it for everyone, clickbait-makers.

602
You get what you get

The vast majority of podcasts are free, so while it's all very well for me to lay down rules saying you should do this and you shouldn't do that, most podcasters aren't getting paid, not in Australia anyway. Which means they can do what they like, and we should be grateful for the free content. As my good friend and prolific podcaster Dave O'Neil often likes to remind listeners, 'You get what you get, and you don't get upset.'

603
Don't treat your friend like a podcast

This is a rule for people who like to call you for chats from their car. Obviously they're bored, maybe they've forgotten to cue up the next episode of their favourite podcast, so why not kill some time phoning a friend? And that's totally fine. My objection is to the way they cut you off the minute they reach their destination. Car-callers should have the decency to park and remain in the stationary vehicle long enough to allow the conversation to reach its natural and polite conclusion.

REALITY TELEVISION

Curiously, the pandemic did not kill off reality television. In fact, much like the radioactive spider that bit Peter Parker, the virus only seems to have made it stronger. Accordingly, I am now obliged to include these rules as part of the actual book, as opposed to relegating them to a special removable section like I did in 488 Rules for Life.

604
No need to recap what happened three minutes ago

Most reality shows now contain as many minutes of recapping as they do of actual content. By all means, recap what happened on the previous episode—no one minds a bit of 'previously on . . . ' work—but it's insulting to assume your viewer can't remember what happened before the commercial break. Stop dragging it out, producers, or more of us are going to switch off and just start reading James Weir's highly entertaining online recaps of your dumb shows instead.

605
Don't top up your fillers right before filming

Remember the camera already adds ten pounds, so if you go pumping additional fat into your face then you are going to look insane. Respect the viewers and stop hurting our eyes. And while you're respecting stuff, maybe respect your own face and how young it is. There's simply no need for fillers when your face is still full of collagen and rubbery youthfulness. I should be looking at you and fighting the urge to press my finger into your cheek so I can watch it spring back like a perfectly cooked sponge. Instead, I'm fighting the urge to google Lady Penelope from *Thunderbirds* to compare whose face looks harder and more plasticky.

606
Stop blaming the edit

I realise they can do a lot in the edit, but they can't make you look like you're shouting and saying stupid things if you didn't shout and say stupid things. That's on you.

607
No kissing until the final episode

The Bachelor should not be able to sample the goods until he commits and makes his choice at the end of the series. As it stands now, the show is less of a 'search for love' and more of an inside look at life with a harem. Week after week we are forced to watch the Bach indiscriminately crack on to every woman in the house. It's like a PG-rated orgy, where everyone lines up in an orderly fashion and waits to tap in. And it's completely gross. It also supports my hypothesis that Covid-19 started not in a wet market but on the set of *The Bachelor Wuhan*. I'm not being a prude and a wowser (well, I am but with good reason), I'm advocating for better television. Imagine if they weren't allowed to slaver all over one another like Kath Day and Kel Knight? There would actually be some unresolved sexual tension in the house (sorry, 'mansion') and therefore, as viewers, we would be so much more invested in the outcome. Who knows, the contestants might even prove to be interesting if they were forced to keep talking to each other and couldn't resort to straddling one another and dry humping the minute they run out of conversation.

Ross and Rachel didn't get it on until season two, episode seven of *Friends*, thus proving my point that viewers are quite happy to wait.

* *Obviously I'm not just talking about The Bachelor, I'm also referring to The Bachelorette, and the idiots on MAFS, and the ones on the island and in paradise; this no-kissing rule applies to all the shows. Except Lego Masters —Brickman and Hamish should definitely kiss every episode.*

A word about the arts industry

It's all too easy to make jokes about 'the arts' not being a real job; I do it all the time. But let's not forget that all the content we've been so voraciously consuming during lockdowns is largely brought to you by the arts and entertainment industry. I'm not, for a minute, comparing artists to frontline healthcare workers, or suggesting we stand outside at 7 pm every night and bang pots and pans to salute musicians and actors and filmmakers for getting us through the pandemic. I'm saying, just spare a thought for the industry next time you skip the credits on Netflix. (No judgement by the way, who doesn't skip?)

At the time of writing, live performance was still largely dormant, to the point where my own tour seems to have been renamed 'Kitty Flanagan—Rescheduled'. And I'm sure I'm not the only performer who'd like to thank anyone who bought a ticket to a show and is still holding on to it. Your solidarity is much *appreciated and I assure you the shows will go on. Eventually. Fingers crossed. No, they will. I'm sure of it. I'm a hundred per cent certain they will probably happen—in which case we might need a couple of rules.*

FRIENDS OF THE SHOW

608
Don't be afraid to lie

Any decent performer knows when things haven't gone great. And what we need after a dud show is a bit of bolstering from our friends; a white lie and a white wine will do nicely. What we don't need are any of those 'clever' avoidance comments. Hoary old chestnuts like: 'Oh my goodness! What about you?' Or worse, 'Oh wow ... so how do *you* think it went?' We're not idiots, we know these things are code for, 'I have nothing good to say about what you just did up there.'

609
A free ticket comes with one condition

When you accept a free ticket to a show, you are obliged to send a text the minute the show is over. Whether it's music, comedy, theatre, whatever—as the lights come up, take out your phone and tap this:

Thank you SO much for the tickets,
we really enjoyed ourselves.

Maybe you hated the show, maybe the band was a train wreck, maybe the comedian paced around so much you got motion sickness—it doesn't matter. You took the freebie and, sadly, nothing in life is truly free. So pay the piper. Send that disingenuous text pronto. If it pains you to tell such lies, then next time don't take the freebie. And if you were foolish enough to accept a free ticket to some performance art, I can't help you; clearly you're a masochist.

ZOOM GIGS

610
Zoom shows aren't fun for anyone

Hats off to the bosses who tried to do something nice for their staff during Covid, like organising a Zoom Christmas party or a Friday afternoon fun session with a comedian as the entertainment. Speaking as the comedian/entertainment at several such events, firstly I would like to thank you for giving me some much-needed work. Secondly, I'd like to offer my condolences to anyone who had to sit through one of these appalling 'shows'. I think it's the closest I've come to feeling like the mad lady who shouts at anyone and no one in particular on a tram or a street corner. In my defence, I will say that it is very difficult to perform stand-up comedy sitting alone at your desk, all the while watching the 'number of attendees' tick down in the bottom of the screen as, one by one, people lose interest and French exit the Zoom party.

SPECIAL PANDEMIC TIMES SECTION
ZOOM ETIQUETTE

Even though I no longer work in an office, I still find myself having to participate in a lot of Zoom meetings. But I know I'm getting off lightly compared to those who are forced to use Zoom on a daily basis—to you people I say, sorry for your loss, you will never get that time back. I spend most of my time in Zoom meetings scribbling notes about how we could be doing it better. That's why there are a lot of rules in this section, starting with the most obvious of them all:

611
Every interaction doesn't have to be a Zoom meeting

Use all the time you save by not commuting to think carefully about whether you really need to have a Zoom meeting. Perhaps an email or a phone call will suffice. Phone calls are an extremely efficient form of communication and, best of all, on the phone it's easier to hide how bored or annoyed you are. Whereas on Zoom you have to constantly smile and nod and look genuinely interested. It's exhausting.

612
No Zooms before 9.30 am

Anything earlier than that is impossible; I'm still stuck commuting from the kitchen to the laundry.

613
Go easy on the jargon

No one wants to 'jump on a Zoom'. People who say 'jump on a Zoom' tend to be the same people who say 'circle back' and 'can you speak *to* that?' instead of 'can you talk about that?' If you use that sort of lingo, please allow everyone extra time to momentarily turn our cameras off so we can all roll our eyes and give the screen the finger.

614
Don't record a Zoom meeting

When was the last time you heard someone say, 'Hey, remember that classic Zoom we had in May 2021 about OH&S? I recall we said some pretty great stuff, I wouldn't mind looking back at it.' That's right, never.

615
If you call the meeting, run the meeting

In other words, have an agenda and get cracking. It's tedious when everyone is present but no one takes charge. Awkwardness prevails as people wave hello to one another and feel obliged to fill the dead air with arbitrary comments like, 'Oh hey, Janice . . . wow, look at you . . . you've got a hat on, is it cold where you are?' Take control and call this wretched thing to order. The sooner you start, the sooner we can all 'jump off' this Zoom.

616
No wannabe pilots at the Zoom meeting

It's really distracting when people don a full aviator-style headset complete with mic attachment for a simple Zoom meeting. I'm sure the sound quality is improved but I just can't take you seriously, Captain. Be sure to let us all know when you've finished your pre-flight checks and you're ready for take-off.

617
Don't angle your screen so everyone
is looking at your ceiling

Or your nostrils. Or the underside of your chin. We're all screen-savvy enough now to know that your camera needs to be at eye level or slightly above. No one expects you to have a full studio set up —just face the light and put your laptop on a pile of books. Think of it as a great way to finally use that stack of recipe books you've never opened.

618
Keep one small corner of your house tidy

Normally during Zoom meetings, I spend a lot of time squinting into the screen trying to work out exactly what's in that pile of crap behind you. Is that clean or dirty laundry in the basket? Is that a dog ferreting around in that scramble of computer leads or . . . a weird-looking baby? I'm not suggesting that you clean up your house, god no, but one of the few good things about Zoom is that you can present as perfectly tidy with little to no effort. Simply push all of your mess to one side and angle the camera away from it.

619
Don't over-style your Zoom background

Tidy is one thing, but strategically placed awards and objets d'art are another. No need to drag potted palms and bowls of feature lemons into Zoom Corner; you want it neat and tidy but not styled for a reveal on *The Block*. Anytime someone comments on your background, you've gone too far. I know, I know, it's a very fine line, and if it makes you feel better, I still don't have it right myself. That's why I really wish we could forget Zoom altogether and bring back the landline. Oh, the landline, such clarity, not to mention that thrilling element of risk during a thunderstorm!

This rule is slightly different if you've been tapped to do a Zoom cross on television. In that case, you want to take some time to stage a visually pleasing and, where possible, relevant set. For example, if you're a doctor, have some doctor paraphernalia in shot; perhaps your degree framed on the wall, or a few medical texts or journals on the desk—just a little something that sets the scene. It's hard enough watching a person speak via Zoom on television; it's even worse when they're sat in front of a bare white wall or a closed venetian blind. This makes it feel less like you're watching an expert and more like you're watching a hostage video.

620
Make jokes at your own risk

The sound quality is terrible on Zoom, so be prepared for your hilarious rejoinder to be met with blank faces followed by 'What?' You'll be forced to repeat what you said, and with every repetition your joke will get less and less funny and you'll wish you'd never said anything in the first place.

621
One hour, no extensions

If you can't get it done in an hour, quit the meeting and have a long hard think about how you could have been more efficient. People have bladders. And short attention spans. Not to mention Netflix and a dozen other streaming services to work their way through.

622
Take a break whenever you need one

Feel free to wander off during a Zoom meeting—after all, 95 per cent of meetings aren't essential anyway, so you won't miss a thing. Just be sure to mute yourself and turn the camera off before leaving the room. That way it looks like it might be a technical issue rather than what it really is—you bored out of your scone and going to the fridge for the fiftieth time to see if anything good has magically appeared in there. When you return and put your camera back on, remember to look concerned and say, 'Sorry guys, don't know what happened there, I lost you for a minute. Am I back? Have you got me?'

623
Make friends with the mute button

Muting allows you to be present in the meeting while still doing other stuff, such as watching something on YouTube or texting your friends. Muting is also mandatory when you leave to take a toilet break. Mandatory.

624
Social Zooms need structure too

Zoom has certainly proved to be an excellent, albeit awkward, way to get friends and family together during these times of forced separation. The social Zoom, however, can quickly run out of steam if you don't have a plan. Once that initial flurry of excited waving at the screen dies down and people have stopped shouting and showing what drink they're having, no one is ever quite sure what to do next. Should you ask a question to the group and watch chaos ensue as everyone tries to answer at once? Or do you direct your enquiry to a specific individual and risk it becoming a private conversation with half a dozen silent observers? Give your gathering some kind of direction by conducting a trivia contest or playing a parlour game. In the case of a birthday, a custom quiz about the birthday person is always a hit. Use the time you would normally take to get ready for a night out to find some trivia questions online, google some parlour games or rip a quiz out of the newspaper. Everyone will adore you for it.

SOCIALISING

CATCHING UP

625
Don't be passive about making a plan

When you arrange to meet up with someone, deciding on where to go can often drag on longer than the eventual catch-up itself. You might think it makes you sound easygoing to chime in with 'Whatever suits you, works for me!' But opting out like that actually makes you really annoying. Admit it, you're being lazy and hoping someone else will do all the heavy lifting and arrange everything. I know that's true because I do it all the time. I don't like the pressure of having to suggest a place to meet up, but guess what? Neither does anyone else. I've realised that it's a bold and admirable act to be the person who suggests where everyone should meet up. It's also smart. Get in first and you can choose locations that are on your side of town or, even better, within walking distance of your own house. Be the first responder of the catch-up plan.

626
First to arrive gets the banquette

Whoever arrives first gets to sit on the comfortable spongy seat against the wall. That's your reward for punctuality. Latecomers must be punished and forced to take whatever on-trend chair substitute is on offer, be it a cold metal stool, a rustic timber stump or an ironically 'trashy' milk crate with or without a cushion. If you arrive at the same time, then you're looking at a *Hunger Games* meets musical-chairs-when-the-music-stops situation. Run, push and shove your way through in order to claim the banquette.

627
Be specific about the catch-up

Take a tip from my good friend and socialising wizard, Julia Zemiro. She occasionally likes to arrange a drinks-meet by keeping it specific: 'Let's meet up for a drink. One sensible drink.' There are so many things to like about this invitation. Firstly, she makes clear she's not suggesting a big night out where we're all going to get wasted and lose our shoes. Secondly, it indicates you should feel comfortable about driving your own vehicle to the meet, no need to uber or worry about how you're getting home. Thirdly, it puts a cap on the night and makes the idea of a midweek catch-up far more appealing. And finally, it leaves you free to honour any other plans or obligations you may have made for later on in the evening. Even if those plans were just to head home and watch your programs and eat that delicious soup you've been thinking about all day.

*   *Clearly this tip is not for anyone under thirty, for whom the thought of capping the night in any way is anathema.*

628
Cancel plans with alacrity

Never be afraid to call and cancel. If you feel like cancelling, there's every chance the other person secretly wants to cancel too. Many people love a surprise cancellation. It might even be one of the greatest gifts you can give. The non-canceller now has a night to themselves *and* the moral high ground, so they can revel in that smug feeling of being the good friend who was 'totally planning to show up'.

FURRY FRIENDS

629
No birthday hats on dogs

In fact, no outfits on pets. Nothing channels a pet's inner sadness like being forced to stagger around 'dressed' as a piece of pizza or a princess. I will make an exception for the costume that turns a sausage dog into a teddy bear running at you—that should be included with every purchase of a dachshund.

630
Pick one up for the team

If you're a dog owner, do the world a favour and occasionally pick up a 'coldie' at the park. To be clear, I'm talking about an old dog poo, not a beer, and not all the time—just every now and then. It's a noble and selfless act to pick up a poo your dog didn't do. You're saving someone else from stepping in it, you're making sure the dog park stays a dog park and you're keeping your own balance sheet tidy. Because no matter how vigilant you are, there has probably been at least one occasion where your dog has plopped somewhere without you realising it. So remember this terrific saying of mine: 'See a dog poo, pick it up, all day long you'll have good luck!'

631
Always state your whereabouts when talking to someone on the phone

This rule is specifically for dog owners when they're out walking their dogs, and it's included at my sister's request. Apparently, she and I were talking on the phone one day but I neglected to mention that I was walking my dogs at the time. So when I shouted, 'Gotta go, there's a poo happening!' and hung up, she had no idea the poo in question belonged to one of my dogs. Rather, she assumed I'd become some sort of chronic oversharer who liked to keep everyone apprised of my movements.

MEETING AND GREETING

632
No more elbow bumping

In Australia we've never had a standardised greeting. Some people kiss, some people double kiss; there are huggers and handshakers and combinations of all of the above. It's a minefield. And now, thanks to the coronavirus, we also have this ill-conceived elbow-bump gesture thrown into the mix. Part chicken dance, part Thai boxing attack, the elbow whack refuses to catch on. For good reason. It looks ridiculous and it's anything but perfunctory. An elbow bump is always followed by a thirty-second postmortem where everyone involved feels obliged to acknowledge how weird and random it is that we have to knock elbows now. No one is capable of just bumping and moving on. You see it whenever politicians gather: they jostle and stump rub each other and narrate the proceedings, 'Heh, heh, alright, no we can't shake anymore can we, here we go, elbow bumping, that's the way, heh heh, ahhhh, that's a bit of fun, isn't it? Good stuff.' Just stop it. We gave it a crack, it didn't work. Let it go.

633
Touch nothing, touch no one

It feels like a good way to greet each other in times of disease would be to channel *Star Trek*'s Mr Spock and do a version of the Vulcan salute. But maybe close your fingers. So you end up raising a flat hand with your palm facing out. It's easy, it's socially distant, and having your hand up like a stop sign conveys a very clear message: 'Halt, come no further, don't share your germs with me.' Although, you'll need to be careful with this one; don't flick it up too casually or it could become less Mr Spock and more Mr Hitler.

634
Announce your proposed style of greeting

When the pandemic subsides and we invariably make a return to the superspreading hugging and kissing combinations of old, I suggest we start heralding our greeting of choice. Let your acquaintance know with a clear announcement what to expect and where to expect it: 'Coming in on the left, single kiss' or 'I'm a hugger, get ready!' This avoids any misunderstanding, and uncomfortable moments like the time I misjudged my uncle's approach and ended up kissing him on the lips.

If you're on social media, you might want to think about adding it to your profile: *Hi, my name is Rodney, I'm a non-hugger and my preferred greeting is a tip of the hat.*

635
Avoid the awkward double goodbye

After a night out, when everyone is standing outside the restaurant or theatre or wherever, about to part ways, before any farewelling begins someone must first ask the question, 'Which way are you headed?' Only then, once people have indicated the direction they're going, should you say your goodbyes. This stops you having your big hugs and emotional scenes outside the restaurant, then realising you're all walking off in the same direction, with everyone thinking, *Damn, do we walk in silence now or do we have to start up a new conversation?* And then having to do a second round of goodbyes.

636
Never introduce yourself by saying, 'You don't remember me, do you?'

It's aggressive and unfair, especially if you haven't seen the person since you went to school with them thirty years ago. No one looks the same as they did at school. And we haven't all been stalking one another on Facebook, so a lot of us are unaware of how people have changed. The correct and polite way to introduce yourself to someone you haven't seen for a long time is to state your name and immediately identify how you know one another. For example, 'Hello, I'm Olivia Jackson, we went to school together.' Or, 'Hello, I'm Sandy, we met at Betty and Kenickie's wedding.' It's a much friendlier way to kick off a chat. A conversation isn't something you need to 'win', there is nothing to be gained by opening with a gotcha moment like, 'Hah, I knew you wouldn't remember me!'

SPECIAL FOLLOW-UP RULE FOR THE MARRIED LADIES

637
Use your maiden name

If you haven't seen someone since school, please use your maiden name when you introduce yourself. Using your married name is perverse and unnecessarily cryptic. If you genuinely want to catch up and converse, then let's dispense with the tedious *Sale of the Century* 'Who Am I?' game up front and get to the chats.

SEXY TAIMES

638
Women like men with a sense of humour, and a neck

Unless you're planning to pull a plough, you probably don't need to overdevelop your trapezius muscles. So take a day off from the traps, guys, don't let your neck disappear. And while you're at it, don't go stupid on 'arm day' or 'leg day' either. It's a fine line between being a Hemsworth and looking like you have an entire family of Very Hungry Caterpillars sticking out all over your torso.

639
Sex doesn't have to be spicy

The compulsion to spice things up in the bedroom is a purely human condition.

No other species feels the need to get kooky and experimental with sex. You don't see lions out on the savannah whipping one another with branches across the hindquarters. The giraffes aren't tapping the elephant on the next plain to have a three-some and I've certainly never seen hippos rolling around in the mud sucking each other's feet—and if there was ever a creature designed to fit a foot in its mouth, it's a hippo. Bears might cover themselves in honey but I'm pretty sure it's a food thing not a sex thing. And even if it was some kind of sticky bear foreplay, they don't have bed sheets and mattresses to worry about. There's no shame in being good at plain sex.

640
No one likes Marathon Man in the bedroom

I'm not suggesting you should be racing to finish a hundred-metre sprint. But a solid 1500-metre performance is certainly preferable to a 42-kilometre endurance event—especially given that you're not offering any drinks breaks, time-outs or half-time entertainment. And this supposedly sexy promise some people like to make of 'I am going to keep you up all night!' That's less of a turn-on and more like a threat they make at Guantanamo.

641
Never tell a woman to calm down

Unless, of course, you're trying to get her to kick right off. I'd suggest using a coded alternative like, 'Perhaps we could have a cup of tea and talk about this some more.'

SPECIAL PANDEMIC TIMES SECTION
SOME SPECIFICS

PANDEMIC RULES FOR BIG BUSINESS

642
Stop telling us we are all in this together

This is a rule for banks, television networks and other large corporations (but mostly banks). Now, more than ever in these 'unprecedented times', you can take your wafty, soft-focus, hand-holdy ads and piss right off. Anyone who's ever tried to apply for any kind of loan or credit or extension from a bank would know there is no hand-holding, there is no understanding, there's certainly no friendly, personal bank manager trained to listen to and assess your individual circumstances. There's only the cent-ralised call centre and the algorithm. They're in this together. And I'm pretty sure they're doing okay.

643
Don't pretend to be my friend

At the beginning of the pandemic, I got a flurry of emails from companies and stores who were all very keen to be my friend and help get me through these tough times. The CEO of Woolworths started emailing me personally and including a picture of himself. 'Dear Kitty,' he wrote, before going on to tell me all sorts of tales about the crazy capers the Woolies staff had been up to that week, or maybe it was that capers were selling at a crazy price, I can't quite remember (he did go on a bit, I think he might have been lonely). Furniture store West Elm also emailed to say they had my back. Thanks, guys! Specifically, they wrote: 'Whether it's keeping the kids entertained or getting creative in the kitchen, West Elm is here to help.' I was delighted. I wrote back to let them know I didn't have any kids but that I could sure use a new sofa given that I was doing a lot more sitting on my arse these days. Maybe my email went to their junk folder, I don't know, but I never did hear back from them.

I guess the clue that these were all friendship scams was there the whole time, in the subject headers that said, 'Do not reply to this email'.

PANDEMIC RULES FOR CELEBRITIES

644
Be careful who you tell to 'relax and enjoy the lockdown'

Many people are not in a privileged enough position to take an indefinite salary holiday. So tread carefully when you talk about how much you're enjoying time with the family and the 'benefits' of being forced to take a bit of downtime.

645
If you get an email from Gal Gadot, move it swiftly to junk

Turns out celebrities singing 'Imagine' acapella while earnestly gazing into their iPhones was not what people needed to help them cope with lockdown. I'm sure Gal's heart was in the right place but, seriously, imagine all the peee-pull (celebrities) who now wish they'd thought twice about agreeing to be part of that mawkish display of desperation and neediness.

AND FINALLY . . .

SOME STRONG SUGGESTIONS

To finish up, I would like to offer some suggestions. These are things that I thought were too obtuse (even for me) to include as rules. But then I thought, maybe I could just strongly suggest them and see what happens.

Throw your mattress out sooner

This suggestion really only applies to a tiny percentage of the population. I'm talking about the people who discard their mattresses by tossing them in back alleys. Setting aside the illegal dumping issue, what is going on with those mattresses? Have you really been sleeping on that thing up until now? I have never seen a discarded 'street' mattress that doesn't look like a crime scene. Every one of them looks like it should have been thrown out at least three murders ago.

No Uber Eats before noon

If I'm completely honest, I wanted to make this suggestion simply 'No Uber Eats', but I dialled it down lest people throw my book against a wall and dump it in a germy street library. I realise my objection to Uber Eats is completely irrational: 'Tonight, I'll be having food that arrives cold and looks like it has fallen off the back of a bike and been kicked the last hundred metres down the road to my house.' Not that I would ever blame the drivers for doing that. It must be such a dispiriting job. Riding around risking your life on a bicycle or moped at night, fetching other people's food, and being paid tuppence to do it.

I strongly suggest patronising local restaurants who have their own delivery drivers or maybe even going to pick up the food yourself (and obviously by 'pick it up yourself', I mean, send your partner or bribe your flatmate to pick it up for you). You'll get your food faster and hotter, and the restaurant will get a bigger cut of the profits. But if you won't do that, could we at least agree that you won't use Uber Eats to bring you breakfast. I mean, come on, how hard is toast?

Don't waste money on specialty boxed chocolates

The routine for eating fancy boxed chocolates goes like this: make your selection, take a small bite, pull a face, then dump it back in its moulded plastic hole and move on to the next one. Eventually you find yourself staring at a tray of half-eaten truffles, fondants and pralines, which you stash somewhere and forget about until the day comes when you're desperate and have no other treats in the house. So you pull them out and do another round of nibbling, face-pulling and discarding.

If you're thinking about giving chocolates as a gift, I strongly suggest wrapping up a classic bar, something like a full-size Snickers or a Cherry Ripe, or even a simple block of Caramello, and if it's someone really special, why not gift them all three? I know if I received a gift like that I'd be rather surprised—but I'd also be delighted.

AND ONE STUPID SUGGESTION

I am well aware that this one is ridiculous, I just thought it might be fun to end the book by hitting a wasps' nest with a stick and running away . . .

Mandatory vasectomies at fifty

Gents, feel free to put the book down, I reckon it's safe to assume you won't like this one. My thinking is that mandatory vasectomies in middle age would be the great equaliser. It might force men to think differently about their relationships if they, too, had a ticking biological clock. Women can't keep having kids up until the day they die so it seems unfair that men should be allowed to keep spraying it around into their seventies and eighties. It's really not fair on the kids either. Imagine being at school when a kid looks out the classroom window and shouts, 'Look! There's an old man in pyjamas weeing on the monkey bars . . . oh I'm sorry, I mean—hey Byron, your dad's here!'

Acknowledgements

It's only a skinny little book but there are always a lot of people to thank.

Firstly, the team at Allen & Unwin: Kelly, Angela, Jo, Dannielle, Garry and especially Simon for accommodating all my last-minute changes! Thank you.

Penny and Sophie—double FBs to you both, it's such a delight working with people who make you laugh hard, there's nothing quite like it.

Tohby, we got there. Once again, you took a plain little book and made it special.

To my readers, Glenn and Bex, thank you for the feedback and especially for the reassurance.

Artie Laing, what can I say? You're the best in the biz.

And a very special thankyou to Monica Johansson, who allowed me to include her banana rule, Liz Winters for her thoughts on TikTok and Sam Pang for teaching me Rule 635.

Most of all, I'd like to say a massive thankyou to everyone who bought the original book, *488 Rules for Life*, and made it such a hit. You are the only reason I was allowed to have another crack at this. Socially distant, air high fives to you all. xx

Index

to *488 Rules for Life* and *More Rules for Life*

Numbers in entries refer to **rule numbers**